BREAKING THE SILENCE
BROKEN TO BLESSED

KERRY ANN RICHARDS

BREAKING THE SILENCE. Copyright © 2024. Kerry Ann Richards. All Rights Reserved.

Printed in the United States of America.

No portion of this book may be reproduced, stored in a retrieval system, or transmitted in any form or by any means, except for brief quotations in printed reviews, without the prior written permission of DayeLight Publishers or Kerry Ann Richards.

ISBN: 978-1-958443-65-1 (paperback)

Scripture quotations marked "NKJV" are taken from the New King James Version. Copyright © 1982 by Thomas Nelson, Inc. Used by permission. All rights reserved. Bible text from the New King James Version® is not to be reproduced in copies or otherwise by any means except as permitted in writing by Thomas Nelson, Inc., Attn: Bible Rights and Permissions, P.O. Box 141000, Nashville, TN 37214-1000.

This book is dedicated to every person, both male and female, boy and girl, who has been through some form of abuse at any stage of his/her life, and to my heartbeat, my son, Jacob Rowe, who will continue this legacy through our Foundation "Voice of the Voiceless."

ACKNOWLEDGMENTS

I want to first acknowledge God Almighty, who made this possible. He gave me the vision years ago but sat on me until my wound became my weapon, which is the voice for the voiceless through every process to make this book possible. I also want to acknowledge my sister, who runs TAPM business services. She prayed with me countlessly when the challenges felt insurmountable and reassured me that God will finish that which He has started in me.

Thanks to my coach and mentor, Crystal and the DayeLight Publishing Team, who worked with my busy schedule to make this book a reality.

Last but certainly not least, and most importantly, thanks to you, my readers, who have chosen this book out of many others so we can all support each other on this mission.

TABLE OF CONTENTS

Acknowledgments v

Preface 9

Chapter 1: You Are Not Alone 15

Chapter 2: You Have Been Heard 27

Chapter 3: Sharing LOVE 31

Chapter 4: Get Connected 35

Chapter 5: Preparation Season 39

Chapter 6: Forgiveness 45

Chapter 7: S.T.R.E.N.G.T.H. 51

Chapter 8: Overcome 57

    Prayer 61

    Conclusion 63

    About the Author 65

PREFACE

For some, the trauma of our childhood resides in the mere shadows of our memory and is only visible in our painful reactions to the life we now live. These painful experiences defy articulation. It is fragments of the past that are easy to keep hidden, and we are hesitant to confront them. It is the story of many persons who have chosen the vulnerability of silence in order to mask the painful reality that haunts our dreams and influences our emotions. This escape, though the more tolerable option, is far from the solution that would cause us to transcend the traumatic experience of being abused as a child.

I choose to embark on this journey of recounting my experience for two reasons: one, it is a part of my process to complete my healing journey, and two, my story can help others who may be going through something similar or have gone through such. Our pain often becomes our testimony. As one rightfully said, "There is purpose in our pain." Our mess can be turned into a powerful and profound message for those who are hurting from a painful past. We can aid

Preface

each other in finding healing and wholeness by breaking the silence.

The language of abuse is a weighty subject to be discussed. For years, the shame of my encounters weighed heavily on my consciousness, and I struggled to find the words to clarify what I felt in my heart. There was much difficulty in choosing to speak out than it was to remain silent, but silence creates barriers that hinders our journey to wholeness. Secrecy cloaks our experiences, allowing society to label such trauma as taboo, and the pervasive culture of victim-blaming conspires to stifle those of us who are survivors, especially the most vulnerable among us: our children.

In retelling my own journey, I often grappled with the memories that I have long buried and had to face head-on the societal dynamics that perpetuate the silence. I encountered the whispers of doubt, the fear of judgment, and the persistent echoes of a culture that often shies away from addressing the uncomfortable truth, adding to the difficulty in opening up about wounds inflicted in the innocence of youth.

This book is a testimony to the courage required to break the shackles of silence. This is me acknowledging the countless others who bear the weight of their untold stories, locked away in the chambers of their souls. As a woman who has navigated the realms of silence, I strive to give voice to the silent struggles, to illuminate the path toward understanding, empathy, and, ultimately, healing.

I pray that my story will light a candle in the darkness, creating a small flicker of light that will give courage to others to share their stories so that together, we can dismantle the barriers that shroud the conversation around childhood sexual abuse. Only through dialogue, understanding, and collective compassion can we dismantle the walls of silence and pave the way for a future where no child feels compelled to carry the burden of their pain alone.

Though I write from the perspective of a woman, I know sexual abuse also affects males. This is an overly sensitive topic for everyone, both male and female, who have experienced abuse; physical, emotional, psychological, or sexual. Since the 1970s, women have been speaking up about sexual abuse based on studies done by the Sexual Assault Awareness by the Washington Coalition of Sexual Assault Programs. Unfortunately, people are still living in secret with abusive loved ones, family members, and even spouses. They are scared because the assaulters are people close to them who sometimes hold powerful positions in

Preface

their community, so no one believes the victims when they speak out. The time has come for us to answer this question, "Why me?" Most victims ask themselves this question, but what we should truly ask ourselves is, "Why not me?" Many of us can go through certain painful experiences because we were built to survive. Our stories then become a testimony to those who go through the same experience but would never survive if not for you breaking the silence.

Let us start by thanking God for choosing us to be a light in the valley of darkness; it may seem like nothing is there for us to be grateful for, but look around you. Through it all, you are still alive and well. Many like us have taken their lives to be free from the bondage they thought would never end, so use this moment to worship no matter your age. God has saved you, so you can use your voice for such a time as this.

Children are often brought up to keep quiet and only speak when spoken to, but not this time. This is the time for you to listen to your children and family members because they have something to say. So many of our children are being abused and are threatened by their abuser to keep quiet. Such silence eats away at their souls like a tapeworm. Enough is enough! I hope I have earned your attention.

You have made a very important step in getting a copy of this book. Parents, guardians, and loved ones, please listen to your children, nephews, nieces, grandchildren, and loved ones when they choose to break the silence because they don't normally trust anyone besides "silence."

CHAPTER I

YOU ARE NOT ALONE

It is difficult to write on this topic without visiting the landscape of my childhood memories. I was not just an observer but a participant in the events that are still fresh in my mind. The echoes of the past reverberate through the corridors of my mind, and each footstep resonates with the weight of my untold stories that will unfold on these pages to reveal a voice that now desires to speak against the evil of childhood sexual abuse.

In muted suffering, the voice of a survivor resonates with the words that will set the foundation for this journey: You are not alone. You were not the first to experience such trauma, and you will probably not be the last. The insidious nature of abuse is often marked by isolation, as though shame and secrecy are bricks in an impenetrable wall. But let this be the first breach in that barrier. You are not alone in your silence, in your struggle to find the words that feel like shards of glass on your tongue. In this shared space of vulnerability, we embark together on a journey to dismantle the fortress of hushed pain.

The journey to break the silence is loaded with thorns, and each step is a testimony to the strength that resides within the very core of the survivor. As we face the emotions, memories, and societal constructs, let us not forget that others have walked—and are still walking—this winding road. Our voices together, though often hushed to a whisper, will swell into a resonant anthem and challenge the silence that binds us.

We begin by acknowledging the countless survivors who have grappled with the weight of unspoken traumatic stories. I invite you to recognize your voice as well; your voice is a powerful instrument of change. When you share your truth, you become a beacon for others who may still find themselves trapped in the suffocating grasp of silence.

Vulnerability is not weakness, and speaking out is not only an act of courage but also an act of resistance. You are not alone, and your story matters. Together, our voices are strong enough to shatter the silence that has for too long obscured the reality of childhood sexual abuse.

Are you tired of crying yourself to sleep? Are you afraid of the day turning into night or waking up three or four times during the night? Are you afraid to be alone with anyone? If any of these questions describe you, then know that you are never alone. Daddy Jesus is always there with you, even though you can't see Him. I know the feeling of despair all too well, but I want you to remember that no matter how alone you may feel physically, God is always there with you. This is His promise:

Let your conduct be without covetousness; be content with such things as you have. For He has said, "I will never leave you nor forsake you." (Hebrews 13:5 - NKJV).

Often when we face a traumatic experience, the world tends to vanish. We can lose sight of the fact that other people exist in this world. Experiencing a traumatic event can have a negative impact on our perception of the world around us. Trauma has a way of consuming our attention and overwhelming our senses to the extent that the external reality may seem to fade away or become distorted. This phenomenon is often described as a sense of the world vanishing or losing its significance in the aftermath of trauma. Trauma can create a sort of "tunnel vision," which narrows our focus to the immediate threat or the intense emotions associated with a traumatic experience. The peripheral elements of our environment, including the presence of other people, may become less noticeable or entirely overlooked.

Trauma also triggers intense emotional responses such as fear, shock or grief. These emotions can be so all-encompassing that they dominate our awareness, making it challenging to connect with the external world or the people in it. The overwhelming emotional burden can create a temporary disconnect from our surroundings. In response to trauma, some individuals may experience dissociation—a coping mechanism where there is a sense of detachment from oneself or the surroundings. This detachment can further contribute to a feeling of the world fading away, as if existing in a detached, surreal state.

Trauma often activates the body's stress response, triggering a heightened state of alertness and a laser-like focus on survival. In this state, our attention may be solely directed towards self-preservation, leading to a diminished awareness of the presence and experiences of others. Traumatic events can disrupt our sense of time and continuity. Past, present, and future may blur together, making it difficult to anchor oneself in the current moment so we can set goals or acknowledge the existence of others who share this temporal space.

Reconnecting with the world and acknowledging the existence of others often requires a gradual process of healing, where the individual can reintegrate their experiences and rebuild their connection to the broader reality.

As I reminisce about my own experience, it was one hot summer evening in July. School was out for the summer. My grandma told me I was going to my dad (the man who grew me) whom I had never met before to spend the summer as I prepared to start high school in September of that same year. I was so excited because I wanted brothers and sisters to play with, amongst getting to spend time with my dad and stepmom, which is different from always being around my grandma and my little brother on my mother's side.

That was the first summer I wasn't going to summer classes in all my life thus far. I would have enjoyed going to summer classes that summer because I would get to meet new friends and teachers, especially since I was scheduled to attend a new school. I was excited about high school. I was now a teenager, and I could start doing things I loved without being monitored by my grandma. Little did I know that my grandma had this plan to send me away for the summer without even letting me know, but I understood because she was getting older and could not manage a teenager like me who showed early signs of a boss mentality.

As I was growing up, I was more and more alone until my mom had my little brother almost eight years later. I realized that it was cool to have siblings and loved ones your age to play with, so I was extremely happy. Regardless, I was happy for the opportunity to go away for the summer, so bags were quickly packed, and I was ready to go any day now.

I got picked up a few days later and taken to my dad. Upon arrival, I noticed some high walls. It felt like I was entering a general penitentiary—which is another name for the prisons in our country—and there was only one way in and one way out. I didn't pay much attention to it because I thought it was just décor. I learned a few weeks into staying there that he intentionally built it like that, and everyone in the area called him "BIG DON," which is another name for area leader.

As young as I was, I started having a weird feeling inside of me because I thought I was coming there to have fun, but it turned out to be like a boot camp, especially when the gate was always kept closed. The first few days were fun. I got to know my siblings and my stepmother who I grew to love. She was like a mother to me. She combed my hair and cared for me. I didn't know much about my dad. I had never spent time with him before then, but based on what I was seeing, he seemed to have money because he had more than one house in the yard. It was a large yard space, and he had a pool, other lands, and businesses too. Being in that new environment was so exciting because I had never had access to anything like that, so my first few weeks were really good.

There is a famous saying that goes like this: "Not everything that glitters is gold," and it is so true. As the weeks passed by, I started seeing my dad's true colors, but I started to tell myself that when a dad loves their children, he will spank them as the Bible mentioned to not spare the rod and spoil the child (see Proverbs 13:24). My stepmother was truly a nice person though and very soft at heart. She treated me like a real daughter, and I had always dreamt of having something like that in my life, so I was right beside her, learning all I could from her. Some of my siblings were a bit jealous, but I didn't care because she was a great person.

The days continued to fly by so quickly. By the end of August, I learned that I had a sister with the same name as me who was celebrating her birthday as well, so all of us were preparing to close out the summer with a two-in-one birthday party, as well as a back-to-school treat for the kids in the community. I felt so blessed to be a part of such a celebration.

Summer ended, and it was the first week of September, which was only days away before the new school year began. It was time for me to return home to my grandma and little brother. I was very sad because I enjoyed my time with my siblings and stepmother. Before heading home, my dad took me shopping to get all my back-to-school items among other personal items. While on our way home, I noticed he was playing with my hair, but I didn't think anything of it even though I didn't feel comfortable, and I didn't say anything. The thing that caught me off-guard was when he kissed me goodbye when I was coming out of the car. I was so shocked that I didn't tell anyone when I got home. I just went to my room and kept replaying the incident in my mind. I didn't know who I could trust to share that with. As children, we were not allowed to speak out of context so I never told my grandmother at all about the kiss or many other things that are too detestable to speak about.

For seven years, I went through abuse as a child. I remember the nights as if it happened yesterday. I remember the squeaking of the door in the silence of the morning. I remember the man who was supposed to be my dad on top of me. This man was supposed to love and protect me, yet he caused me the greatest harm in my life. But he was not the only one who inflicted the scars I bore in my body. I was abused by older brothers and a taxi driver who was there to take me to school. I went through a cycle of abuse as a child, and when I thought it was over, I got pregnant for him, but he couldn't take the shame so he brought me to the family doctor to get an abortion. I am breaking the silence once and for all for every child, teenager, young adult, and even grown adults who has or is going through some form of abuse. It is time to speak up and speak out.

Children, do not be afraid to speak up. Tell someone; Tell your Guidance Counselor if a family member is touching you inappropriately. If you stay silent, it only gets worse.

I remember nights when I used to go and sleep beside my younger brother to escape my abuser. I would get beaten to go to my room because female's rooms were different from where the males were. I told my younger brothers what was happening, but they were too young to understand and couldn't even help me if they wanted to. A caregiver tried to help me, but her words fell on deaf ears.

Parents, do not turn a deaf ear to the cries of your child. Guardians don't turn a deaf ear. Don't be that parent who turns a deaf ear because of the money coming in. Pay attention to your child. Observe their body language because sometimes they can't say what they want to say. Listen to your child. Take the time to know your child.

I remember days when I prayed that the night would not come. My God. There were days I would do anything for it not to get dark because I knew after certain hours that someone would come into my room. Abortions became a sign and scar of my childhood trauma.

Speak up! Your abuser can't hurt you anymore. My abusers robbed me of my childhood. I didn't know what it was to be a regular child; to have a daughter-father relationship. I didn't know what it was to play like regular children. I was so scarred that I had poor choice of men when I wanted a relationship. I ended up picking the wrong men looking for love in my earlier years. When you never experience true love, you settle for anything that looks like love.

Stop running! Someone is waiting to help you, so speak up about that abuser. Don't allow them to have power over you anymore. Speak up!

It's not about you.

Let it out. The road to recovery is not easy, but we have many tools and resources now at our disposal. But there is no help for you unless you break the silence. You have a community; you have a foundation. **Voice of the Voiceless Foundation** was created for you. It is a safe space for you to live in, for you to breathe, for your voice to be heard. So let it out.

Give it all to God. Jesus died so you can be free. Raise your voice for every child who has been abused. Raise it for the young adults who have been abused. Let's break the silence.

I can tell you that you are not alone because I was right where you are years ago. It started with weekend visits to permanently living in a broken home where I was the bait for their lustful and detestable sins, which became so overbearing. When I spoke out, I was badly beaten because they ensured that no one listened to me, so everyone had me as a liar. When we find ourselves in such a situation, often the abuser doesn't want anyone to listen to you. If you're reading this book as a parent or guardian, I encourage you to listen to your children. They may not make sense at first, but please listen to them and watch their body language.

You Are Not Alone

You are not alone anymore, so speak up, my fellow girls and boys, young adults and adults overall. Do not be afraid. This is the message God gave me to give to you. He says, "I am your voice; speak up, break the silence." I break the silence over your life. When you walk into rooms, you will own the room, and when you speak, people will listen attentively.

Break the silence of fear. Speak out from the pain. I know school can become a haven when there is trouble at home. You may be afraid of day turning into night when school is out. I know the silent cries when the whispers of the night get darker and the door is silently pushed open. I know the anguish when your mouth is covered by your screams, so today, I am saying to you that you are never alone. Speak to your guidance counselor; speak to your teacher, and teachers, please observe your students. You can also reach out to my team at voicesconsultingser1@gmail.com.

Break the silence and speak to someone, anyone, and when it feels like no one is listening, remember that God is with you always. He will never leave you nor forsake you, so please take Him at His Word. Break the silence because you are not alone and together, we are going to break the silence off the generations to come. Tears is a language only God understands, so cry if you must, but break the silence right now that has robbed you of your childhood for far too long.

CHAPTER 2

YOU HAVE BEEN HEARD

The clock keeps ticking as society moves forward, oblivious to what often goes on behind closed doors and veiled whispers. There is an insidious plague that lurks in the shadows—the silent suffering of countless souls who bear the weight of untold stories. But now there is a resounding echo that pierces the stifling silence: You have been heard.

Acknowledging the existence of this pervasive darkness is a crucial first step. Here we acknowledged the unheard cries, stifled screams, and muted pleas that reverberate through the lives of survivors. Every paragraph written here is a testimony to the courage needed to shatter the shackles of silence and confront the negative impact of child sexual abuse. We live in a world where vulnerability is often perceived as weakness. I extend a compassionate embrace to those who have endured the unthinkable burdens of abuse.

You are not alone. You have been heard. Your experiences are validated, your pain acknowledged, and your voice is granted the space it deserves.

Breaking the silence is not only about unveiling the horrors that fester in the shadows, but it is about affirming the resilience of the human spirit. The journey towards healing begins with the understanding that, in sharing your story, you refuse to be defined solely by the pain inflicted upon you. You reclaim your narrative, and in doing so, you invite others to do the same. Your voice is not just a sound in the void but a catalyst for change. When you speak out, you become a beacon of hope for those who are still provoked to silence. The words "You have been heard" resonate with a promise that the collective "we" are here, listening, learning, and advocating for a world where the silence surrounding child sex abuse is shattered and replaced by a chorus of voices demanding understanding, justice, and healing.

What does "hearing" represent to you in this season? Hearing is listening to the spoken and unspoken words of that inner voice and certainly that of the Holy Spirit. I know there are times you cry alone, wondering if God is hearing you. Sometimes you may become so angry at God for allowing such a degrading deed to be done to you in the height of your innocence, but know this: tears is a language only God understands, so cry, bawl, weep, and mourn until you have emptied all that pain from your spirit so you can start receiving what God has in store for you. His Word reminds us:

Come to Me, all you who labour and are heavy laden, and I will give you rest. Take My yoke upon you and learn from Me, for I am gentle and lowly in heart, and you will find rest for your souls. (Matthew 11:28-29 - NKJV).

In our deepest pain, we must learn to listen and hear that still, small voice. We all have that inner child in us where we are afraid to say the wrong thing or do the wrong thing without being judged, but today, I say to you, your voice has been heard louder than you had expected it to be, and help is here. Help is on its way to you right now, so just take that step and break the silence.

Don't you ever for a moment think that God doesn't hear your cries or that He has forsaken you. The one thing we can count on every second, minute, and hour is that He will never leave us nor forsake us. He is faithful and just to keep His Word so remember that God has stored all your tears in a bottle for all the hurt you have gone through and is going through, and He will certainly repay all those persons who have wronged you.

You Have Been Heard

I was there—where you are—years ago. I was afraid, lonely, and wondering if God was hearing me and when He would send help. I questioned myself, "Why did I have to go through all of this hurt?" One day I heard a song on the radio playing, "I just say YES, Lord, lead the way," and from that day, I never stopped letting the Lord lead me. Today, I am asking you to just let go and let God do it for you because He has heard you—You have been heard!

Let today be the day your chains break off from your hearts, lips, hands, and feet so you can stand boldly and say, "I am not the person I used to be yesterday or last year." Let your voice be heard from the deepest valley to the highest mountains that you are more than a conqueror in Christ Jesus. They can't hurt you anymore because God has heard your cry, and help is here. Help is on its way, and it will always be available when you need it.

Time surely heals all things; I am not saying it will be easy, but I can safely say that you will find comfort in Jesus because no counsellor or mortal person can help you through these difficult times like Jesus can. Dry your tears now, my child, and believe me when I say that God is going to work it out for you in ways no human can ever understand and rescue you as He did for the three Hebrew boys in Daniel 3:26-28.

CHAPTER 3

♡

SHARING LOVE

After a child's innocence is broken, a deep journey begins that goes beyond the pain, shame, and troubling memories. Sharing love is a key part of this road toward healing; it is the start of a life-changing journey, a choice to break the cycle of silence and sadness that surrounds people who have been sexually abused as children. It is a call to reclaim one's humanity, make connections, and find a way to get better.

When someone breaks your trust, love in its purest form can heal the scars. It makes people stronger and give them the tools to deal with the rough waters of their feelings. By showing love, we recognize that every survivor has value, and that their identity is not based on the tragedy they went through. Survivors are not defined by what they went through. Connecting and sharing with each other can heal your wound faster. It looks at the different ways that love can show up, such as in supportive relationships, therapy, and the power that comes from survivors coming together. Sharing love is not just about romantic or familial relationships; it is about everything that makes up a person. Compassion and understanding become the threads that hold recovery together.

People need to be brave enough to show love to survivors of sexual abuse. Survivors need friends who will always be there for them, maybe a therapist who can provide a safe place to talk, and supporters who are working hard to get rid of the social stigma around sex abuse among children.

It is also important to love yourself because survivors deserve the same kindness they show to others. You have the strength to learn to love yourself again and free yourself from the chains of guilt and shame that may have been holding you back. Love has the power to turn pain into strength, loneliness into connection, and silence into a resounding chorus of voices demanding healing and justice.

For God so loved the world that He gave His only begotten Son, that whoever believes in Him should not perish but have everlasting life. (John 3:16 - NKJV).

Jesus dying on the cross reflects how much God loves us and that He sent His only begotten Son into this world to save a sinner like us. I know it is very hard to accept love after what you have gone through, much less to share love with others, especially with those who hurt you but as of today, I want you to first accept Jesus' love for you, then start to love yourself whole-heartedly because you are fearfully and wonderfully made (see Psalm 139:14). We need to be grateful to the Lord for loving us, and then slowly we will automatically start to love even those who wrongfully use and mistreat us.

Open your heart to love others like yourself. No one said it would be easy, but it will get easier with time. Start trusting Jesus and learn to depend on Him more as you pause to think about why you should love those who hurt you. Ask yourself, "How many times have I hurt others and God, and they still love me?" Do you want God's forgiveness? If your answer is yes, then you must love your enemies—truly love them—and forgive them for what they have done to you so you can start the healing process.

And forgive us our debts, as we forgive our debtors. And do not lead us into temptation, but deliver us from the evil one. For Yours is the kingdom and the power and the glory forever. Amen. For if you forgive men their

Sharing Love

trespasses, your heavenly Father will also forgive you. (Matthew 6:12-14 - NKJV).

Think about the fruit of the Spirit that Paul wrote about:

But the fruit of the Spirit is love, joy, peace, longsuffering, kindness, goodness, faithfulness, gentleness, self-control. Against such there is no law. (Galatians 5:22-23 - NKJV).

The key here is love.

And above all things have fervent love for one another, for "love will cover a multitude of sins." (1 Peter 4:8 - NKJV).

Love covers the multitude of sins, so start today and every day onward by loving others, even when they do not deserve it. You will start feeling the peace of Jesus in your soul, mind, and body.

Owe no man anything than to love them. (Romans 13:8).

CHAPTER 4

∞

GET CONNECTED

The lifeline for survivors of child sexual abuse is being able to traverse from being a victim to becoming an empowered person. Being connected is about the deep process of connecting with one's inner power and making a strong bond with it in order to heal from trauma. People who have been abused often feel broken afterward, like the very core of their being has been violated. Still, deep inside, that broken self is an incredibly strong source of power. Being connected means starting an in-depth study of this inner reservoir. It means realizing that, despite the hurts, there is a strong core ready to be found again.

While they are healing, survivors form a deep bond with their true selves. This means facing the pain, fear, and weakness that may have been hidden deep inside with courage. It takes both kindness and determination to get

Get Connected

through this trip as survivors slowly reveal the depths of their feelings and find the strength that has always been inside them. This journey is about self-discovery and self-acceptance, which can change your life. To connect to your inner strength, you must accept your feelings, even the ones that hurt, and welcome the road to self-love. Survivors can take back control of their story by reflecting on it. Push past that toothache and take action by finding strength. They can find strength in being vulnerable and resolve to be kind to themselves.

Many have suffered abuse who, in their darkest hours, found an unknown depth within themselves—a safe place where healing and freedom meet. This profound transmutation comes about when you get back in touch with your personality after a traumatic event and build a sense of health that goes beyond the scars of the past. Some therapeutic approaches and routines can help with this inner connection. Survivors are encouraged to try a variety of methods that help them connect with their inner selves in a healthy way, such as breathing techniques and creative arts. The path to healing is not a straight line, so it is important to be patient and kind to yourself as you go through it.

What do I mean by connected? Start to connect to your inner being with that higher self or Supreme being called the

Holy Spirit. When you accept Christ as Lord and Saviour, you will start feeling that spiritual connection the closer you get to Jesus. Connection to the Holy Spirit is beautiful and one which is not easily explained to persons who are not yet born again.

I know what it feels like to be disconnected from everyone, particularly yourself, wondering and wishing you were not born, especially in the family you now are a part of. It is hard to accept the reality of what we went through and wonder why this has happened to us and not someone else. Many have gone through sexual abuse; many have been spared the trauma. We don't know why God allows such atrocities to happen to children, especially those who are vulnerable and often unable to defend themselves. But one thing is sure:

And we know that all things work together for good to those who love God, to those who are the called according to His purpose. (Romans 8:28 - NKJV).

If you have been through any form of abuse or know anyone who went through abuse, you can share this book with them, while as you read on, I pray for your strength and deliverance so you can come to complete healing. A healed soul is an empowered soul. Someone is depending on your victory testimony in order to come out as pure gold. Once you connect to the right source, your healing is inevitable.

How can you make this connection? You can start by accepting Jesus Christ, then start reading His Word (The Bible) which is a guide to connecting to Him every day of your life onwards. Don't be ashamed, disheartened, or feel worthless. Jesus can turn your mess into a message. I am a testimony of this. God used my pain to birth books and a charity organization that will help children and young adults, just like you. We also cater to the needs of grown adults, male and female, who are broken from a similar situation, so start right now by accepting Jesus and you will witness this connection that I am talking about.

Don't give the abuser any more power over your life by not being connected to anyone. That is what the devil wants. His goal is to steal your joy and peace of mind by convincing you to remain silent and feel like no one loves you. Enough is enough; get up and get connected to God, yourself, your family, peers, and other people in your community. God loves you so much that He sent His one and only Son, Jesus, to die for you, so get connected and stay connected to the blood of Jesus, your loved ones and your voices community at large.

CHAPTER 5

PREPARATION SEASON

For I know the thoughts that I think toward you, says the Lord, thoughts of peace and not of evil, to give you a future and a hope. (Jeremiah 29:11 - NKJV).

The "preparation season" is an important part of healing. It is when survivors of child abuse get over the haunting memories of their past and become strong advocates ready to break the silence that traps so many others. From being a victim to a champion is a big change, like getting ready for a season where your experiences, pain, and strength come together to make a strong force for change. Survivors go through this life-changing phase, learning about themselves, healing, and gaining power. In the end, they find a way to help others break free from the crushing grip of silence.

Preparation Season

During the preparation season, people face the hard parts of their past and break down the walls that used to keep them inside. The focus changes from just surviving to intentionally building resilience—resilience that helps others find their way through the shadows of their own tragedies. Survivors find their way through the depths of their feelings and write a story about their experiences that goes beyond being victims. They embrace a new identity that is based on power and purpose.

Survivors think carefully about their own trip during the preparation season, which is a time for self-reflection. They find the strong lines that run through their lives and recognize how much they have changed from being victims to survivors to advocates. As survivors rise from the ashes of their past, they become walkers of light who show others the way. We have the power to take back control of our lives and help those who are still stuck in silence. Child abuse victims can bring about change by educating others, raising awareness, and reaching out to others. They can break the cycle of silence that surrounds the problem of child sex abuse.

There are many ways that people use their pain to do good. Whether through lobbying work, support groups, or art, survivors turn the preparation season into strength that inspires others to find their words and break free from the chains of silence. When survivors come out of this season of change, they bring with them the experience and knowledge they gained along the way. The preparation season turns into a holy place, a furnace where the strength built up inside becomes a light that guides those who are still walking in the dark. It shows how strong the human spirit is—how it can rise from the ashes, unbroken "as a caterpillar" that is transformed to a free-spirited butterfly that is ready to help others and bring about a new day of knowledge and healing through perpetual resilience.

God says, **"I know the thoughts that I think toward you…thoughts of peace and not of evil, to give you a future and a hope."** As simple as it sounds, it is one of the most powerful scriptures in the Bible. It speaks to all our generations before and after. Embedded in this text is a purpose that no one can abort because we are chosen for such a time as this. Let your pain be your inspiration for others like you to know that no matter what they are going through, God is still the beginning and the end, and this too shall pass.

Let these additional scriptures be your source of strength and deliverance:

Surely goodness and mercy shall follow me all the days of my life; and I will dwell in the house of the Lord forever. (Psalm 23:6 - NKJV).

Do not fret because of evildoers, nor be envious of the workers of iniquity. (Psalm 37:1 - NKJV).

The Lord said to my Lord, "Sit at My right hand, till I make Your enemies Your footstool." (Psalm 110:1 - NKJV).

The book of "**Daniel**" is also a good book to read.

Stop giving yourself headaches and sleepless nights over what has happened to you in the past. Yes, I know it is easier said than done, but start rejoicing for what is to come through this inspirational season. This is your winning season because everything and everyone that was sent to destroy you will witness the restoration of the Glory of God through you.

"So I will restore to you the years that the swarming locust has eaten, the crawling locust, the consuming locust, and the chewing locust, my great army which I sent among you. You shall eat in plenty and be satisfied, and praise the name of the Lord your God, who has dealt wondrously with you; and My people shall never be put to shame. Then you shall know that I am in the midst of Israel: I am the Lord your God and there is no other. My people shall never be put to shame. (Joel 2:25-27 - NKJV).

And the Lord restored Job's losses when he prayed for his friends. Indeed the Lord gave Job twice as much as he had before. Then all his brothers, all his sisters, and all those who had been his acquaintances before, came to him and ate food with him in his house; and they consoled him and comforted him for all the adversity that the Lord had brought upon him. Each one gave him a piece of silver and each a ring of gold. Now the Lord blessed the latter days of Job more than his beginning; for he had fourteen thousand sheep, six thousand camels, one thousand yoke of oxen, and one thousand female donkeys. He also had seven sons and three daughters. And he called the name of the first Jemimah, the name of the second Keziah, and the name of the third Keren-Happuch. In all the land were found no women so beautiful as the daughters of Job; and their father gave them an inheritance among their brothers. After this Job lived one hundred and forty years, and saw his children and grandchildren for four generations. So Job died, old and full of days. (Job 42:10-17 - NKJV).

Preparation Season

Your praise is your weapon. Smile and praise your way through and your victory will be sweet. You are more than a conqueror through Christ Jesus. Every time you feel discouraged, read the above scriptures again and speak these words to yourself: *You are the head and not the tail; you are above and not beneath; you are a lender and not a borrower because you are royalty in Christ Jesus.*

And the Lord will make you the head and not the tail; you shall be above only, and not be beneath, if you heed the commandments of the Lord your God, which I command you today, and are careful to observe them. (Deuteronomy 28:13 - NKJV).

CHAPTER 6

FORGIVENESS

Taking a journey on the road of forgiveness is like going into uncharted land. It is hard, but it will deeply free you. Let go and allow God to lead you through this life-changing process. It will be hard, but I promise it will be one of the best choices you ever make. In the process of forgiving, let us not confuse love and forgiveness because they are not the same thing. The Bible makes a very important point clear:

And above all things have fervent love for one another, for "love will cover a multitude of sins." (1 Peter 4:8 - NKJV).

It is impossible to deny the presence of God in your life when you engage your heart, mind, and body in love. God is love. Love is an act of God, and so is forgiveness. Forgiving someone gives you real peace—an inner calm that goes

Forgiveness

beyond what people can understand. Although forgiving someone is indeed difficult, it is also important to remember that learning God's way is the only way to truly accept forgiveness. Forgiveness is not for them, the abusers, but it's for you. It is not easy to go on this path, but it is the only way to truly forgive others. We also access our forgiveness by forgiving others.

Some people may question why they should forgive those who have hurt them. Think about how many times you have sinned against God and asked Him to forgive you before you think about this question. The truth can be found in this self-reflection. You can start to heal by forgiving others, and you have been forgiven. Forgive those who have caused you pain in any way. Release the hurt; release them. Apostle Paul's circumstance is a good lesson on this:

And lest I should be exalted above measure by the abundance of the revelations, a thorn in the flesh was given to me, a messenger of Satan to buffet me, lest I be exalted above measure. Concerning this thing I pleaded with the Lord three times that it might depart from me. And He said to me, "My grace is sufficient for you, for My strength is made perfect in weakness." Therefore most gladly I will rather boast in my infirmities, that the power of Christ may rest upon me. Therefore I take

pleasure in infirmities, in reproaches, in needs, in persecutions, in distresses, for Christ's sake. For when I am weak, then I am strong. (2 Corinthians 12:7-10 - NKJV).

Paul tried to get rid of the thorn in his flesh. God responds by saying His GRACE is sufficient. When you want your problems to go away, remember that God will strengthen you enough to get you through it. God has not brought you this far only to leave you now. May these words change the way you think as your relationship with God grows. Even when you are in a lot of pain, God is always working for you.

Forgiving someone who has hurt you is not a gift for them; it is a gift you give to yourself. Giving everything to God allows Him to work in you in a new way. Letting go of what you know and accepting what you don't know is part of spiritual growth. You must believe that the God who knows the future will lead you, no matter how scary the road ahead may look. As you go through life, forgiving others become a key that opens the door to a new spirit, a healed heart, and a free mind. Take advantage of this time to let go and let God. This life-changing act holds the key to a fresh start— a path to peace, healing, and God's kindness showing up in your life.

Forgiveness

Forgive them. I know it is easier said than done. I can testify to that. I had a mild heart attack a few years ago from unforgiveness in my heart. I harbored hatred in my heart. I was bitter towards my parents. My mom didn't even know what I was going through. Forgive quickly. It is not for them; it is for you so you can have peace and enjoy what the Lord has in store for you.

Forgiveness is a very important aspect of the human experience. It can change the life of both the victim and the offender. There are many sins that love can cover. Your spirit, mind, and body are all surrounded by God's holy presence during this life-changing event. Forgiveness gives us a true peace that goes beyond human understanding. When we start the path of forgiving, we begin the healing process.

Sometimes, it is hard to forgive others, but learning to forgive in a way that follows God's ways is the key to truly forgiving others. Applying the same kindness and forgiveness that we receive from God opens the door to a big change. This change starts with forgiving ourselves and then spreads to those who may have caused our pain. As we go through life, forgiving becomes a strong story that changes who we are, renews our spirit, and frees our soul. As we enter this season of letting go and letting God, we enter the life-changing power of forgiveness—a path to peace, healing, and the real presence of God's grace fully manifested in our lives.

I was challenged by God to call my abuser years ago, and I kept ignoring it, thinking that I had forgiven them, until God challenged me with the task. I was getting ready for work one morning when the Holy Spirit said, "Call him." I was acting like God was certainly not talking to me, but when the Holy Spirit said it again, I was like, "Lord, I don't have the number." Can you believe I was trying to give God excuses?

God downloaded the seven digits of the phone number in my spirit, and I smiled and made the call. It was very nerve-racking at first because it was the first time in years that I spoke to him. I told him what God told me to tell him, "I forgive you." He was there asking me what he had done to me. I smiled and said, "Take care of yourself." I felt a dead weight drop off my shoulders when I hung up. I thought I had forgiven him, but God saw that I didn't until that morning when I was released from that dead weight.

Days after that, God tested me again to see if I was truly healed when one of my favourite cousins embarrassed me with the scars of my past. I smiled and worshipped even more because God had truly healed me. My wound is now my weapon and a voice for others like you, so I thank God for truly healing and delivering me so I can run with the vision He gave me years ago to be **"The Voice of the Voiceless."** Because of Jesus, we can be reading this amazing book on how we are overcomers of our past hurts and traumas.

CHAPTER 7

S.T.R.E.N.G.T.H.

Beat your plowshares into swords and your pruning hooks into spears; let the weak say, 'I am strong.' (Joel 3:10 - NKJV).

Out of the abundance of the heart, the mouth speaks (see Luke 6:45). Additionally, Jesus makes a profound statement:

And do not fear those who kill the body but cannot kill the soul. But rather fear Him who can destroy both soul and body in hell. (Matthew 10:28 - NKJV).

The age-old question of why God allows bad things to happen to good people, especially children, is a mystery debated for centuries with no apparent and satisfying conclusion. Yet, the Bible is clear that what a man can do is limited only to the body. He cannot touch our souls or our

S.T.R.E.N.G.T.H.

hearts, and that is where our resilience and strength emerge from.

Being strong may sound irrelevant to others, but you are stronger than you think you are. The challenge for me was to remain strong around others when I was dying inside. Can you relate? Dying is a spiritual term for children who have been to hell and back and remain smiling on the outside; only God alone knows how we do it. On many occasions, our story falls on deaf ears when we share what is happening, and we often feel like a failure and even doubt ourselves, but I want you to know that you are not a liar or a failure. I believe you, and I believe in you. You are a very strong and courageous person who hasn't realized your own strength yet; it will soon manifest and be put to the test even more, so trust the God inside you.

I pray that God will strengthen your body with the same strength He gave Elijah so you can push through all the adversaries and keep your head held high. I know it is a heavy load and a great burden to carry on your shoulders, but please remember that God's grace is sufficient in your weakness, and there is nothing that God will not do on your behalf. Below is a breakdown for you to recite even after you finish reading this book:

S—Serve
T—Thankfully
R—Relatively
E—Earnestly
N—Non-Negotiable
G—Growing
T—Truthfully
H—Honestly

= STRENGTH

Getting over the trauma of being sexually abused as a child is a deep and brave journey that takes an enormous amount of strength and resilience. Even when going through unbearable pain, the human spirit is strong enough to not only live but also triumph over the ghosts of the past. Remember, we are built to last like the Palm Trees in Psalm 92:12, which have the Cedar of Lebanon that never breaks even when it grows over eight feet tall. People who have been sexually abused as children show amazing perseverance that goes beyond the scars they have. These survivors' ability to bounce back shows how strong they are on a deep level, that their terrible experiences don't limit their strength but instead help them heal and gain power that far supersedes their lifetime, which is demonstrated in their generational wealth and legacy they leave behind, like books, foundations, and family businesses for years.

S.T.R.E.N.G.T.H.

It takes courage to face the trauma of being sexually abused as a child. Survivors must face their worst memories and deal with the pain, shame, and fear that often come with them. The strength comes from being ready to face those memories head-on and break down the walls of silence that have kept them locked up. Letting go of control is a sign of strength. Surviving people know that to heal, they need to be open and sensitive with people they trust and get professional help. It takes strength to remove the layers of defense built up around the pain, and I can attest to that. It took me years to trust people because I used to always think the worst of them until I was fully healed. I started to realize that we are all human and we are going to be hurt and hurt others unintentionally, but with GRACE, let the light of understanding and kindness be our inner strength to tear down the walls of brokenness that the enemy trapped us in for far too long.

Survivors show strength by realizing they can't handle things on their own. Asking for help is a sign of self-empowerment and an understanding that healing takes more than one person working together. A lot of people take their pain and use it to make the world a better place. They use what they have been through to become champions, teachers, and supporters, breaking the silence and giving hope to others who may still be dealing with abuse. To turn personal pain into a source of energy, you need to be very strong.

One of the best things you can do for yourself is to change the narrative. Rewriting your story is a sign of strength that can help you get over being sexually abused as a child. People who have been survivors actively change who they are, going from being victims to being a strong person who writes their own stories. It takes strength to face the past and see a better future and work toward it.

Sexual abuse survivors have an inner strength that comes from the very core of their being and shines through in the face of unthinkable hardship—being strong means recognizing the pain, facing the trauma, and getting through the dark parts of the past by being vulnerable. I want you to pause and open your spirit to receive all that the Lord has for you. Stop relying on your physical strength and learn to tap into the strength of the Holy Spirit so you can walk bolder, knowing that you are lighter than before. Weeping may endure only for a night; yes, I know you may be saying your nights are too long, but just remember that everyone has a different length of time, and joy always comes in the morning.

S.T.R.E.N.G.T.H.

Reading this book alone takes strength, courage, and a willingness to end the spirit of silence that has been robbing your peace of mind for years now. I want you to declare with every fiber of your being, "I am free, in Jesus' mighty name." You are indeed FREE.

Therefore if the Son makes you free, you shall be free indeed. (John 8:36 - NKJV).

CHAPTER 8

OVERCOME

We were not created to survive the issues in life but to overcome them. This is what it means to be "More than a conqueror." What God is saying about us is that we will walk away victorious, and the lessons we learn from the experience will make us stronger, wiser, and even more resilient. Each experience prepares us to transition into our next season, and our greatest days are always ahead of us. This is why Paul says:

Brethren, I do not count myself to have apprehended; but one thing I do, forgetting those things which are behind and reaching forward to those things which are ahead, I press toward the goal for the prize of the upward call of God in Christ Jesus. (Philippians 3:13-14 - NKJV).

There is a greater and more glorious reality ahead of you for you to be consumed with what is behind you.

Overcome

What have you overcome? As I was writing this chapter, the Holy Spirit placed this song in my heart, "My shackles are broken. I'm delivered. I've been set free." Look up this song by Jermaine Gordon, and I pray that as you listen to it, you will be released from anything and everyone that has been trying to befall you all these years so you can become an "overcomer."

These things I have spoken to you, that in Me you may have peace. In the world you will have tribulation; but be of good cheer, I have overcome the world." (John 16:33 - NKJV).

It may feel like nothing to you, but you are an overcomer. Jesus already forewarned us that we would go through some unpleasant circumstances, but as He has overcome this world, so can you. You overcome by breaking the silence that has crippled you for far too long. When you look back at where you are coming from, you will see clearly that you are more than a conqueror over that situation, so it is time to remove the band-aid from that wound and let God truly heal you.

Don't let fear, doubt, and vengeance hold you back any longer; let it end today. You wouldn't be here today if you didn't overcome all the negativities that the enemies have set to drive you crazy. Today, accept all the fruits of the Spirit:

The fruits of the Spirit are love, joy, peace, longsuffering, kindness, goodness, faithfulness, gentleness, and self-control. Against such, there is no law. (Galatians 5:22-23 - NKJV).

For me, I struggled with self-control for years because I held on to the hurt longer than I should, until that day when God truly healed me. I don't get upset easily anymore, and I forgive quickly and keep it moving so I can demonstrate the fruits of the Spirit through me. Keep this in mind; healing is for you, and overcoming is for you. You are the greatest benefactor, so get up, put one foot in front of the other, and keep it going— *"God's got you!"*

Remember, as you try to define if you are an overcomer, remember this powerful declaration that God has spoken over your life:

And the Lord will make you the head and not the tail; you shall be above only, and not be beneath, if you heed the commandments of the Lord your God, which I command you today, and are careful to observe them. (Deuteronomy 28:13 - NKJV).

Overcome

Stop feeling guilty because you did nothing wrong. Before you were formed in the womb, God knew this was going to happen to you, so use this lesson to open your mouth to Jesus and cry out to Him three times. Tell Him how you are happy that He died so you can live through this ordeal and show the world that He has helped you to walk out victorious.

I close this chapter with this song "Mercy" by Elevation & Maverick City.

PRAYER

Heavenly Father, I submit our scars and our pain to You. I pray for everyone reading this book: every child, teenager, young adult, parent or guardian, destiny helper; Mighty God. I pray for a touch, that Your people will be bolder and begin to speak up about their abusers.

Mighty God, break that cycle of abuse. Break those generational curses. Turn their scars into a message of triumph. Turn those years of suffering into shouts of praise and joy. Father, I bring the children, parents, guardians, counselors, and anyone reading this book before You and ask that You give them the courage to speak up. Please give them the strength to speak up without being afraid. Assure them that their abuser can no longer hurt them. They have no power over them. Bless these families. Break every curse. Set the captives free.

Father, release every child-like spirit within every person who has gone through abuse. Let all the hurt go RIGHT NOW. I decree and declare you will be set free in the name of Jesus. Thank You, Jesus. Thank You, Holy Spirit. Thank You, Heavenly Father. Thank You for Your revelations. We give You all the glory; we give You all the honor. Thank You for keeping us in our right minds, and shielding us with the breastplate of righteousness and girding us with the whole armor of Your protection, Mighty God. What the enemy intended for evil, You have turned it around for our good. Jesus, cover our minds. Grant us wisdom, knowledge, and understanding. Purify us through Your blood.

Thank You, Lord, for aligning us with Your purpose and for turning our epic mess into a divine message of hope, healing, restoration, and salvation. Do it again, Jesus, as we break the silence on abuse against children, teenagers, both young and grown adults, in Jesus' precious name we pray. AMEN!

CONCLUSION

In concluding, let us embrace ourselves for a season of new beginnings and new blessings like never before. I leave this song with you: "It's a new season, it's a new day. Fresh anointing is flowing YOUR way" by Israel Houghton.

Additionally, here are a few questions I want you to ask yourself and answer as honestly as possible:

1. Are you ready to break the silence of abuse and the abuser?
2. Are you ready to forgive yourself and the abuser?
3. Are you ready to accept love and share it with others?
4. Are you ready to truly live your best life?
5. Are you ready to let go and let God do a new work in you?
6. Are you ready to accept Jesus Christ as your personal Lord and Saviour?

If you answer yes to all of the above, feel free to reach out to me at my email address voicesconsultingserv1@gmail.com, along with all other social media angles so we can pray with

Conclusion

you and connect you to the Voices Consulting Team who will coach and mentor you in the most confidential way possible or get with a local church near you and learn about accepting Jesus as your Lord and Saviour.

As you are about to close this book, do not go out of God's presence. Fast, pray, ask God to direct your path from this day forward, and trust Him to do just that for you.

Thank you for sharing your space with me as we take this journey on the new road to recovery. It's a plan of the enemy for you to remain silent so don't make your silence make you miss what God has in store for you.

ABOUT THE AUTHOR

Kerry Ann Richards is bold and resilient, a fighter for God's people. She is a Kingdom Ambassador for Christ who hails from the parish of Clarendon & is the mother of a handsome young man. She lives by the motto, "God will qualify those He called & where He commissions you He will make Provisions so Step Out in Faith!

Made in the USA
Columbia, SC
30 October 2024